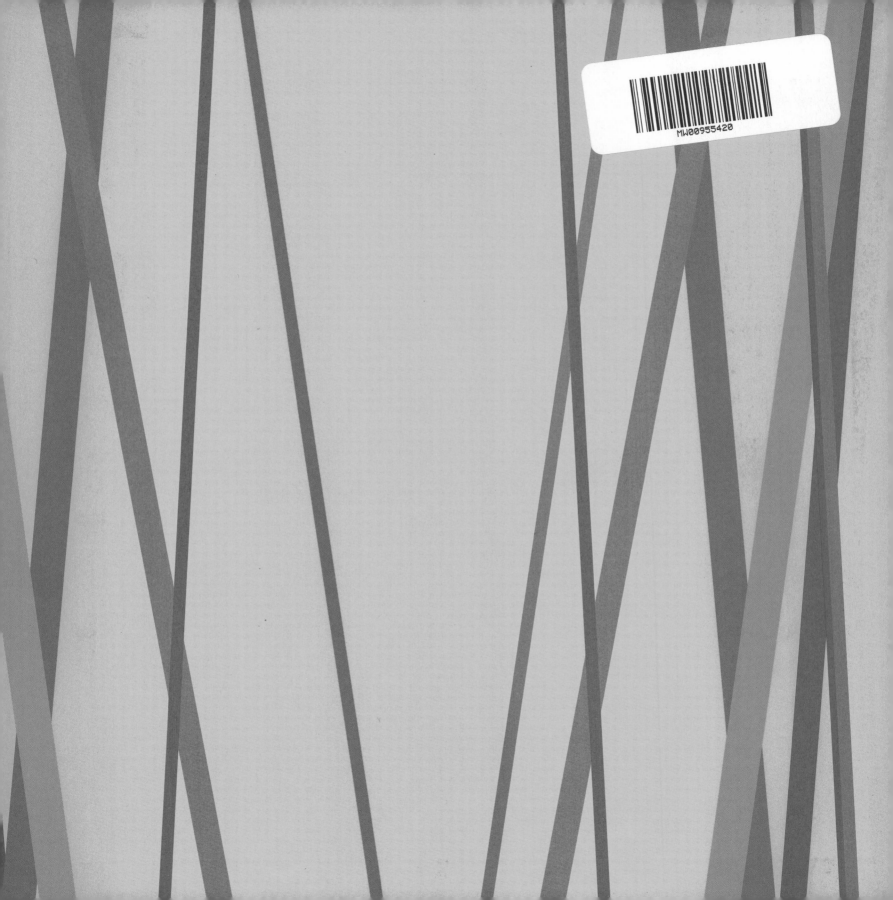

With love to our little angel, Zach
~ Mimi

THE WISE ANIMAL HANDBOOK

Kate B. Jerome

ARCADIA KIDS

Attempt new skills from time to time.

Just try to think them through.

And if you **find** you're left **behind....**

...then change your point of view.

Try **not** **to** **think** of just yourself.

Invent new ways to share.

Stay **close** to **friends** whom you can **trust.**

But
always
be
aware.

Avoid the tattle in the tale.

Insist that truth is best.

Embrace with pride the strengths you have.

Demand
to be
impressed.

Enjoy the peace that nature brings.

Ignore what's just for show.

Join forces when the road gets rough.

Admit when you don't know.

Remember **family** is the **best.**

Despite the **ups** and **downs.**

Don't **hide** from things that you must **face.**

Make
joyful
laughing
sounds.

Eat **healthy** food to **grow** up **strong.**

Be **patient** with your friends.

Try not to take a stubborn stand.

Be
quick
to make
amends.

Excuse
yourself
when
manners
slip.

Be **helpful** every **day.**

Keep **trying** even when it's **hard.**

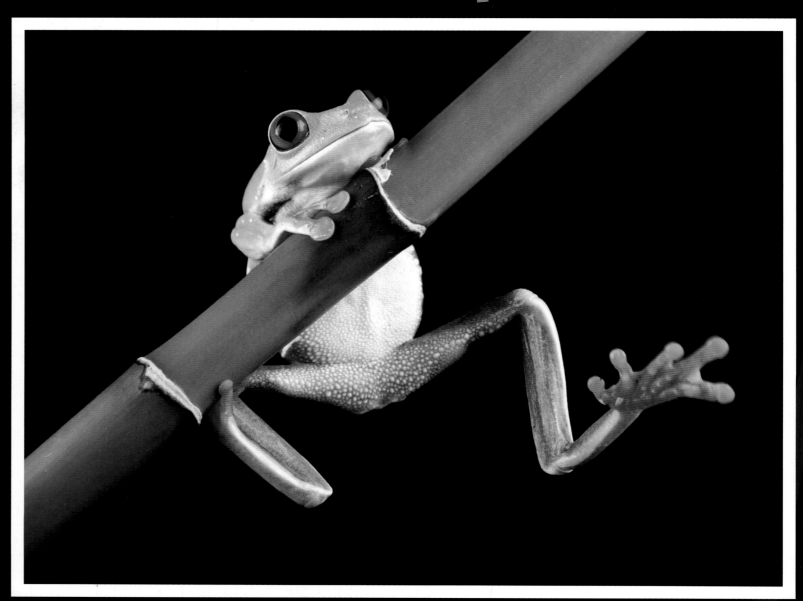

But don't forget to play!

And
sing

...and **dance** each **day!**

Written by Kate B. Jerome
Design and Production: Lumina Datamatics, Inc.
Coloring Illustrations: Tom Pounders
Research: Eric Nyquist

Cover Images: See back cover

Interior Images: 002 Anetapics/Shutterstock.com; 003 George Green/Shutterstock.com; 004 Sergey Uryadnikov/Shutterstock.com; 005 Gnomeandi/Shutterstock.com; 006 Bruce MacQueen/Shutterstock.com; 007 Henk Bentlage/Shutterstock.com; 008 M.M./Shutterstock.com; 009 Mikael Damkier/Shutterstock.com; 010 Brendan van Son/Shutterstock.com; 011 Michael Pettigrew/Shutterstock.com; 012 StevenRussellSmithPhotos/Shutterstock.com; 013 Pakhnyushchy/Shutterstock.com; 014 Patjo/Shutterstock.com; 015 Quinn Martin/Shutterstock.com; 016 Lincoln Rogers/Shutterstock.com; 017 Dirk Ercken/Shutterstock.com; 018 Karel Gallas/Shutterstock.com; 019 Orangecrush/Shutterstock.com; 020 Guenter-foto/Shutterstock.com; 021 Janecat/Shutterstock.com; 022 Shironina/Shutterstock.com; 023 Annette Shaff/Shutterstock.com; 024 Vitaly Titov/Shutterstock.com; 025 Rohappy/Shutterstock.com; 026 MattiaATH/Shutterstock.com; 027 Otsphoto/Shutterstock.com; 028 FikMik/Shutterstock.com; 029 Four Oaks/Shutterstock.com; 030 Ekaterina Kolomeets/Shutterstock.com; 031 Hugh Lansdown/Shutterstock.com.

Published by Arcadia Kids, a division of Arcadia Publishing and
The History Press, Charleston, SC

For all general information contact Arcadia Publishing at:
Telephone: 843-853-2070
Email: sales@arcadiapublishing.com

For Customer Service and Orders:
Toll Free: 1-888-313-2665
Visit us on the Internet at www.arcadiapublishing.com

Library of Congress Cataloging-in-Publication data is on file with the publisher.

Printed in China

Utah State **Animal**

Rocky Mountain Elk

© Kate B. Jerome 2017

Read Together

The Rocky Mountain elk was named the state animal in 1971. Rocky Mountain elk can be spotted on most mountain ranges throughout Utah.

Utah State Bird

California Gull

Read Together

The California gull was named the state bird in 1955. It is thought that this kind of gull saved the crops of early Mormon settlers in 1848–1849. How? The gulls ate the crickets that were destroying the crops!

Utah State Fish

Bonneville Cutthroat Trout

Read Together

The Bonneville cutthroat trout was named the state fish in 1997. This fish is native to Utah and was an important source of food for pioneers and Native Americans.

Utah State Insect

Honeybee

Read Together

The honeybee was named the state insect in 1983. A fifth grade class at Ridgecrest Elementary School in Salt Lake County asked lawmakers to consider the honeybee for this top spot!